Serene Light

Sharing love and light from one family to another.

Serene Baby

This book is a collection of poems written from the heart, shared with courage from mothers, fathers and children from my community.

"Owning our story and loving ourselves through that process is the bravest thing that we'll ever do" – Brene Brown

Dedicated to 'Our Mum' the greatest light, lost in our family.

Table of Contents

LOVE **8**

My Eternal Sunshine 9

The Moment 10

A whirlwind 12

Mine 14

I Love 15

My Sun 16

Are my girls enough? 17

My Motherhood 18

Omg... I've turned into my Mum! 20

Without him...A Dedication to My Husband 21

You Chose Me 22

Motherhood 23

Your 1st Birthday 24

Baby Bear 25

Our days 26

I Wonder? 27

THE FINAL PUSH 28

You are enough 29

I NOW KNOW 30

Mummy's fairy tale 31

LOST LOVE **32**

I'm Alright 33

Benjamin 35

Wonder what you would have been 36

Sweet Mother of Mine 37

My Firstborn Daughter 39

Loss 40
Ruhi – my poem to my unborn lost child (lost through a missed miscarriage) 41

COURAGE   46
3 became 4 became 3 47
Sleep or no sleep 49
Reactive or proactive 51
Numb 52
UNSPOKEN 53
Finding yourself again 54
Do not cry 55

BE BRAVE   56
Believe 57
Finding peace in motherhood 58
I know its hard Mama 59

A JOURNEY   60
You and Me 61
Protector 62
Never Give Up 65

A FATHER'S LOVE   68
Being a Papa 69
Only we can relate 70
Strength 71

A CHILD'S VOICE   72
My childhood 73
I Love You 74

LOVE

My Eternal Sunshine

You are the morning sun;
Each day I am grateful for your presence:
The warmth you radiate
Spreads joy across my face
And fills my soul with bliss.

How your shine casts away life's shadows
And makes each day more brilliant,
Each night, more enchanting
As I wonder at the mystery of the universe,
That gave me such a thing as you.

Love is not a word that does you justice:
To me, you are life itself —
A perfect embodiment of all that is right.
You are my beginning and my end;
My eternal sunshine through the endless night.

An original poem by Melissa Brannlund

The Moment

The moment you held my finger so tight,

An abundance of love so overbearing and hard to describe.

Your heart beat inside me, those very first kicks,

Though you'll no longer fit in my lap, my baby you'll always be.

The moment you held my finger so tight,

That thick black hair, those big brown eyes.

My daughter I knew you were an old soul,

As you grow into a beautiful girl with a heart of gold.

I love you, your free spirit and zest for life,

Oh baby girl, live life to the full and we'll watch by your side.

Watching you put your mark on the world,

How lucky those are yet to meet you,

Your benevolent heart, my first born, my special girl.

The moment you held my finger so tight,

That button nose, tiny toes and bright eyes.

My son, my baby, you stole my heart;

Your inquisitive mind, you are a young soul,

So playful, so new, so full of joy.

Your mind reaches heights, yet your hand stays close.

You will grow taller and look down at me one day,

But you will forever be my baby, my little boy, who stole my heart that day.

The moment you held my hand that day,
I remember the feeling like it was yesterday.
You were meant for me and me for you,
We go back a long way, lifetimes and beyond
The love I have for you gets stronger each day
My hero, my soul mate, my husband, my friend;
Stay by my side until the very end.
Deena Gill

A whirlwind

You came into our life,
Making us a family of four.
Fitting in like a jigsaw puzzle,
Causing no trouble at all.

We had our struggles, I won't tell a lie,
It wasn't all smiles and giggles.
The temper that raged and spilled over in you
No way to calm all those niggles.

I never though this phase would pass
And wondered what I had done wrong
As I cried and worried every day
Wondering how long this would last.

But slowly and surely I see the light
And notice you are changing
I can see your personality through
You no longer show me such a fight.

You come to me and snuggle in close
Wanting to be picked up and hugged.
This I will do any time and day
As I can feel my heart being tugged.

Your little hand reaches for mine

And I love having this connection.

All my worries melt away,

I look down at you and see you are perfection.

Sareena Sinda

Mine

Not my eyes

Has my cheeky glint

Not my mouth

Has my smile

Her heart,

That's all mine

I grew her

I carried her

But she saved me

Pauline Josen

I Love

Little arms wrapped around me,

How you come and have a snuggle

Your little hand no matter what

Always reaches out for mine

Hands clasped together

Fingers interlaced

Arms swaying

Connected in this moment.

Watching you grow up

Wanting time to pause

You will always be my baby

My little kudoo.

Sareena Sinda – Mummy to Krishan Sinda

My Sun

My Sun, you brighten up my day,
When you sleep, I watch you as you lay,

I am so blessed, to have you,
Even though, you do some smelly poos,

I don't mind, because you're perfect to me,
I see us grow, our family tree,

You make me proud, little egg of mine,
A seed you were, you just needed time,

To grow from a pip into a baby,
From a woman to a Mum, is what you made me.

I thank you for teaching me lessons on patience,
When I hold you & we breathe, it becomes a synchronisation.

I am your Mum & you are my Son,
You are my World, my Moon & my Sun.

You are Akiro, meaning Bright little Boy,
Life without you, there would be no Joy.
Lots of Love Mummy xXx

Sapna Colapietro

Are my girls enough?

A beautiful baby girl again…
But are you enough?

Ten tiny fingers, ten tiny toes
A beautiful healthy baby
But are you enough?

C-section scars still fresh
But questions of, will you have another?
Why?
Are my girls not good enough?

Phone calls and messages hesitate to congratulate
But why are you hesitating to celebrate?
Are my girls not enough?

My sweet little girls
You were worth the wait
We loved you at first sight

You are loved
You ARE enough

MKH

My Motherhood

I sit here and wonder what does motherhood mean?

I suppose it's different for you and for me.

For me it's the joy that started 14 years ago, as I watched for the first time my pregnant belly grow.

Aged 19 I wondered if I had made a mistake, but knew this was a decision I had wanted to make.

I felt fear, I felt joy and many hours were spent wondering...are you a girl or a boy?

She was born in March 2006, and from then on there were no more conflicts. All fear was replaced with so much joy, and everyone had thought we were having a boy!

Sleepless nights ensued it was hard I can't lie, I look back and wonder for her did you try?

Mistakes have been made, I for certain am not perfect, but hope I have always made you feel the sacrifices were sooo worth it!

14 years you wished for a baby sister or a brother, so many tears through the years when we tried so hard for another. You're so blessed to have one I would say to the mirror, pretending to accept our clan wouldn't be getting any bigger.

August 2019 a date for my op, "we need to do a pregnancy test before we give that cyst the chop" my heart sank because I had done so many with hope, only to feel heartbroken when the test said nope.

But life was about to change, I couldn't believe my eyes, was this a sick joke or a wonderful surprise? I stared so hard at the words on the screen, pregnant? Are you certain you're talking about me? But a miracle had happened, you're little brother starting to grow, soon my second pregnant belly started to show. Fast forward some months and he's finally here, our miracle baby born in this crazy weird year!

- Lucy

Omg... I've turned into my Mum!

Those dreaded words "You will be just like me, when you're a Mum"

Now I realise Mum, you were right!

Sometimes when I open my mouth my Mother comes out!

"Will you put your clothes away, the house is a mess, the gas cooker needs cleaning"

When I wake up in the morning, all I'm thinking about is how much cleaning I've got to do, oh the laundry, what shall we eat today?

And then I think..."Omg, I've turned into my Mum"

It's never ending! I get it now Mum!

I understand why sometimes you were moody after work,

I get why you kept asking us "what do you want to eat?"

I understand why laundry was such a big deal!

Now that I'm a Mum, I get it!! And those dreaded words "You will be just like me when you're a Mum"

Well...I don't dread it, because I'm proud to be like you!

I am my Mothers Daughter!

Leena Patel

Without him...A Dedication to My Husband

Motherhood has made me cry,
Made me question...
Am I good mother?
Motherhood has been testing,
Where my strengths have been become my weaknesses,
Motherhood has been a constant juggling act,
It has been impossible to keep all the balls in the air,
Motherhood took me to a dark place....

But without him...I would not have found the light,
Without him I would not have got through the struggles,
Without him I would not have got my confidence back,
Without him there would be no one to wipe my tears,
Without him I would not have found love for Motherhood,
On a journey that sometimes feels so lonely,
I realised quickly that I have everything when I am with him!

Leena Patel

You Chose Me

Your soul, your heart, your body grew inside of me,
How magical a woman's body can be.

Your beautiful eyes, your cute button nose, your contagious smile,
How can you be mine? I love you loads.

Your laughter, your charm and your cheesy grin,
What did I do to deserve a perfect win?

I fell in love with you when I first saw you in my tummy,
Thank you for choosing me to be your mummy.

Kim Saini

Motherhood

Motherhood, the biggest gift in life,

My dream especially after becoming a wife.

Everyone has a different birth,

No one can prepare you or predict your story but you know you're lucky if your child gets to walk this earth.

Watching and waiting for each milestone,

Questioning, worrying & googling everything on your phone.

Your smile, your cuddles, your belly laugh, your kisses & more,

Every single aspect of you I adore.

Half of me & half of papa,

I always knew you were going to look dapper.

You've shown me how strong I am and made my dreams come true,

Forever I love you my little blu.

Jessica Bonadies-Stefanoudaki

Your 1st Birthday

There were days that went on forever,
And others that passed in a blur.
A year is a long time for some,
But not when spent with her.

Time has never gone faster,
At a time I wish it would stall.
Your smile, your laugh, your cheekiness,
I'm pleased I've seen it all.

You're beautiful, special, unique;
You're all that I adore.
It's now your one year birthday,
And I couldn't love you more.

Happy birthday little one,
I hope you have the best day.
It's all about you, my darling,
In every single way.

Jessamy

Baby Bear

Good morning baby bear,
What shall we wear?
Sometimes I let you choose,
Then I catch you trying on my shoes.

When you play with a new toy,
I can't help feeling full of joy.
I don't mind tidying up your toys,
I don't even mind all of the noise.

Time with you is so much fun,
Especially when we're out in the sun.
I encouraged you to walk,
And now I'm teaching you to talk.

I love it when we lay on the rug,
Especially when you snuggle in for a hug.
When you splash around in the bath,
Neither of us can help but laugh.

I hold you close and you listen to my heartbeat,
I tickle your belly and kiss your feet.
At night when you want to sleep,
You cuddle up with your beloved sheep.

Fiona Magorrian

Our days

Grateful for your smiles,
Even though sometimes mine is missing,
Grateful for hearing mummy repeatedly
Although it seems like I do not listen.
Grateful for the busy days
When I am constantly invited to play,
Grateful for the sleepless nights
Because only I can keep monsters at bay.

In quieter times, when you're sound asleep
And I find time to reflect,
I come to realise our days,
Are simply our version of perfect.

All I ever wanted, is to be a mum,
Filling our moments with memories
With the best yet to come
You both keep my heart
And hands full
For that, I'll be,
Forever Grateful.

Elena

I Wonder?

Before your birth I wondered.
Baby girl or little boy
I wonder if it's me that can
fill the rest of your life with joy

I wonder what you're thinking
as you stare directly back into my eyes.
Is your heart at bursting point?
Full of love and pride like mine?

You potter around the house
finding things to play and do.
What are you imagining?
I'm in awe while I'm watching you.

Our communication can be silent.
One glance and it all makes sense.
That's family, unity, our tie and bond.
All that our love represents.
Looking into the future ,
I wonder what it holds.
Peaceful times to hustle and bustle.
I'll be with you, as it all unfolds
Elena Mardell

THE FINAL PUSH

The final push,
The aroma of surgical instruments sounds the room
When your hearing is lost
Nothing can be heard, but the grunt from within
Starved of food, the sour taste within my mouth
Parched lips, tired eyes closing, the feeling of nought
And then I hear an almighty cheer
"she's here, she's here"
 but my ears do not hear
Waiting for that high-pitched cry,
the sound that finally makes me cry
tears rolling down my dry cheeks
heart pounding like drumming beats
as she is placed with so much grace
her heaviness pushes down onto my chest
oh my, my baby girl is here
I look down to see this gift from God
That is looking up to me with such awe
Wondering where the hell she has come!

@Bal.kaurc

You are enough

No one need validate you
nor your feelings
nor your thoughts
nor your actions

You are enough
Just the way you are
Have faith in yourself

You know who you are
Look inward rather than outward
You have a whole lot of power
Within you
It is where you actually reside
Tap into your powerhouse

@Bal.kaurc

I NOW KNOW

I now know that I need to put myself first

I now know that I am my number one priority

I now know that it starts and stops with me, that the only one letting me down, is me

I now know that no matter what I do, it may not be enough for those around me

I now know that expectations are not me

I now know that I am more than what I believed to be, that the women inside me, is as beautiful as can be

I now know that is it safe to be me

I now know that it is not a sprint but a marathon, and yes, it's still ok to be me

I now know that this is not the end, this is the beginning and my work is yet to come to a head

I now know I have much more to give, to help humankind, we are in this together, and it is all going to be fine!

@Bal.kaurc

Mummy's fairy tale

9months seemed to take so long,

Mummy was tired, sore, slow to move & unable to do all the things she once could. 9months carrying you, protecting you and preparing for you, felt like a lifetime, but mummy knew you would change her world & be a beautiful happy ending.

Your birth, 5 days in hospital, again seemed to take so long! The hardest thing your mummy has ever had to do. There were scary moments where we feared we'd lost you, or that Mummy couldn't go on - but you arrived and were placed on mummy's chest, with a head full of jet black hair & soft, pale skin. Mummy's little Snow White.

Mummy knew she would do anything for you, you came home and mummy had a list of things she wanted to do! Some silly; setting up your tipi & and some important; feeding and creating a routine, and most importantly having all the snuggles & planning adventures whilst we cuddled.

Mummy's beautiful snow white grew strong, and wild; cooing, smiling, turning, rolling, crawling and now walking and talking a little! Your snow white looks changed more to Alice from Wonderland as your hair grew blonde and your cheeks grew out! Mummy's beautiful fairy tale evolving everyday with every look, adventure and challenge that came our way.

Mummy's loves you and will be here for you as you grow older and need her in a different way. Excited for new milestones, and new adventures, our fairy tale continues little one.

Kirsty, mumma to Autumn Jones

LOST LOVE

I'm Alright

I'm alright. Well, that's what I tell them.

I'm alright because, I'm not even sure myself how to describe what I'm feeling inside.

I'm alright, for you, because I understand that you don't understand so "I'm alright" is easier than trying to make someone understand because you'll never understand so… I'm, alright.

I'm alright and truthfully I feel I have to be, because I know society isn't prepared for me to say what I've got inside of me, so I'm alright spares you the silent awkwardness when you don't know what to say, so hey, I'm alright.

I'm alright because I have no choice but to persevere because truthfully the world doesn't care. And even when it does it's temporary, because everyone's world keeps turning, but mine is still, but I'm alright for those to help their positive energy flow while my negativity grows.

I'm alright because I don't want you to pander, your words of rehearsed kindness do not fill me with joy and hope. I actually wish you would say nothing at all.

I'm alright, because saying you'll be there when I say I'm upset and actually being there is tough, and I don't want you to feel a pressure that you can't maintain.

I'm alright truthfully, but deep down I'm not. It's a persona that I use because really I'm protecting myself, because my hurt gives outsiders ammunition to prey on my weakness.

I'm alright because I don't want to be your talking point at tea with your other friends. My life is not a conversation for others.

I'm alright for many little reasons too many to list, but when you ask someone how they are remember this. Don't make yourself the reason why somebody has to hide behind fake smiles and coffee dates - because I've just lost my child.

So...I'm not alright, and that's alright because I've got it under control. But don't be shocked if I burst into tears, because for me this news is not "old".

Rosie

Benjamin

I have two sons, one with me but one no longer here,

Pregnant with my second child, the end was so near

But just like that, the dream was gone, our wishes torn away,

That magical first hold, every mum should have on that day,

Instead your hit with frightening news that's too much for the mind to take,

Your baby is sick, really sick and all you can do is shake,

You feel naive, you never knew for the 9 months of pregnancy,

No one knew, not a consultant or midwife could see how sick he would be,

6 short weeks spent with him, no time at all,

His health was like a roller coaster a constant rise and fall,

Until the struggle got too hard and it was time to say goodbye,

I couldn't bare to see you suffer, but not sure I could see you die,

Holding your child whilst he's letting go, you should never have to do,

He was so peaceful, we did our best, that I really knew,

The last breaths taken and just like that it stops,

The pain and suffering ended as my tears continue to drop,

The trauma continues long and hard as people have their say,

You paint your smile for others and keep your feelings at bay,

I'll forever have 2 sons, no matter what others see,

My son with me is Christopher and in the sky is Benji.

Chris

Wonder what you would have been

My unborn twin I miss you every day,

I wonder whether you would have been a girl or a boy.

I know the lord needed you and it's why you couldn't stay.

I still wonder what you would have been.

Not a day goes by I don't wonder what colour hair or the colour of your eyes would be,

Whether you had your dad's nose, mouth or would you have looked like me.

I still wonder what you would have been.

Would you be like your brother? Smart funny and loud,

Either way I'm sure you would have made mummy proud.

I still wonder what you would have been.

Although we never met mummy loves you so much,

Oh.. What I would do just to have that first touch.

I still wonder what you would have been.

Just know my little one I will never forget you,

Your siblings think of you too.

We look forward to the day we meet again,

Until then this pain will always remain.

Kayleigh Vernon

Mummy of 5 and 1 angel child

Sweet Mother of Mine

Dear Mum

You plaited my hair in pretty ribbons.

Dressed me in floral frocks, that you hand stitched on your sewing machine.

You gently put surma in my eyes.

Working two jobs, to make sure we were all comfortable.

When you were at work, I used to drag my feet coming home from school, knowing you were not at home.

But when you had a day off, I would run home so quickly.

Knowing I wouldn't have to make cucumber and salad cream sandwiches again.

As I approach the alleyway on the way home, the amazing smells from you cooking come drifting through.

I enter the door way and a feast awaits, homemade chunky chips and fried sausage rolls.

Your chicken soup, I can still taste it now.

Lovely smells of cupcakes will fill the whole street.

On Saturdays we would walk to the post office to get my magazine Tammy, not forgetting a quarter bag of pear drops and your favorite peanut brittle.

Sneaking in bubble gums, you loved blowing bubbles.

Picnics in the park were fun, stacks of parathas and pickle, washed down with masala tea.

Not forgetting banana ice cream lolly pops, with gooey toffee in the middle, they were our favorite mum.

As I got older, I gave you the helping hand you needed with the chores around the house, making things easier for you.

Mum it was nice to see you relax and enjoy the fun time with us all.

For 59 years I loved you mum,

You were the best,

You were superwoman.

Even a clip round the ear did not go a miss.

Mum you taught us well.

Life began with waking up and loving my mother's face.

Love you Mum

xx

By J K Nandhe

My Firstborn Daughter

At 17 weeks you were just too small,
My precious baby,
I couldn't believe my world was about to fall

In the hospital I had to give birth,
I prayed for a miracle,
I would have moved heaven and earth

I watched you die in my hand,
I wished God would take me instead,
Will anyone else ever understand?

You had my hands, my nose and daddy's chin,
Such a beautiful girl,
I was completely broken deep within

I helped lower your coffin into the ground,
Laying you to rest,
With family and friends all around

When I die we'll no longer be apart,
My very own little angel,
Until then you'll stay in my heart

Fiona Magorrian

Loss

Loss…
It does not get easier

The pain does not go away
Not a single bit
But you just learn

Learn to cope with it
As time goes by
You cope with the pain

@Bal.kaurc

Ruhi – my poem to my unborn lost child (lost through a missed miscarriage)

The miracle that was not
The truth that was not.
The love that could not be
I lost you and I am sorry for that.

The pain cannot be explained
The feelings are a-mix
Who do I confide in?
No one saw you – But me!

I know the joy of your coming was short-lived
My health did not support you
I know my mixed feelings were confusing
But my heart still prayed and loved you

I knew something was not right
But I did not want to believe it
Your beginnings were a joy
Of the future, of your life,
of what you would mean to us all

The joy I started to imagine

You were to be our second child
a ray of hope, love, and luck for us all

Seeing your beating heart
beating away
made me turn into mush
I was so glad you were
On your way

I did my best to serve you
Take care of you, feed and protect you
Yet, I could not succeed at it all

The words "I'm sorry… no heartbeat"
Finished it all
Just finished me off!

The two weeks I carried you
When you were actually no more
Felt like a million days
Of hell on Earth

I thank my stars for the support I got
I managed to come out the other end
I am regretful I never got to say goodbye
Nevertheless

The whole process was a nightmare
I cried, I cried… I cried.

I do not think I allowed myself to deal with it all
I just got busy, moved on
Well, that is what I thought it was

The flashbacks came
Your beating heart
The guilt, the pain
I am sorry, I miss you
How do I get rid of this feeling?

I am just so busy
Cannot even think for a second
My life just does not allow me
To deal with my emotions

I pray your soul is at peace
I hope you did not suffer any harm
May God bless you
And you little heart

I am just me, neither perfect or great
I feel anxious all the time
Feeling I can no longer parent the same

The anxiety comes and goes
The feelings a mixture of all
How the hell do I get out of this
This rut…. This hole!

I am sorry… I am sorry
I just do not know what else to say
How do I deal with this loss?
No one can really help me on my way

I am not sure how I should be feeling
Is this feeling normal or ok?
Maybe I need some more time on my own
To work out the way.

@Bal.kaurc

"Courage isn't having the strength to go on – it is going on when you don't have strength." – Napolean Bonaparte

COURAGE

3 became 4 became 3

She came into our lives and I thought our world complete,
But I didn't see you turning away and leaving it behind.
Our perfect daughter, sister to our son,
So small, so innocent, so sweet.
But I didn't see you pulling away and leaving us behind.

Just like that our 3 had become 4.
I made our future plans....

But you never took to fatherhood,
Although I know you tried.
It just didn't come naturally, and it was something you couldn't hide.
But as one child became two
I didn't see you start retreating inside.

But then I saw you leaving,
I watched you walking out the door.
Our perfect baby girl lay sleeping,
as the world closed in around me,
and I lay broken on the floor.

Questions raced around my mind-
How do I carry on?
How do I tell my children that their Daddy has gone?

Just like that our 4 became 3
And I had to make my future plans....

Everything became a blur of heartache, pain and loneliness.
New Motherhood is tough
But adding heartbreak nearly killed me.

I kept reliving that memory,
Kept seeing you walk out that door.
kept seeing you leaving me,
Kept seeing my dreams walk out the door.

But bit by bit I pulled me back together again,
I knew I had to be stronger,
I knew I would get through it.
My perfect little family needed me.
And I had to find my path.

Months have past, our children are doing well.
They are happy, content and full of life.
And though my heart may still be mending I know it's full of love,
because even though you walked away I'm still thankful everyday.

My family may just be 3 but it's all the 3 I need.

Sara - Jane Foster

Sleep or no sleep

I will get through this
It won't last forever
This time will pass
Sleep will return

Sigh!

Parenthood comes with its trials and tribulations
It comes with its lack of sleep
Trying to keep going – whilst being sleep deprived
It's been two years now

Come on!

Trying to stay present
Stay in the moment
Whilst all my mind keeps telling me is
I want to be on a beach –
alone
Sleeping
In the heat
Sunshine
Not having to worry about
Breakfast, Lunch or Tea

This time will pass

This too shall pass – they keep telling me

Sleep will return

One day

I pray!

@Bal.kaurc

Reactive or proactive

You can plan you day
But it doesn't mean
It will be your way

Sometimes instead of being
Proactive
We are left being only
Reactive

But it's ok
Plans change

Just keep your focus on what
Is important
Your health
Your family's health

The rest can wait!

@Bal.kaurc

Numb

I feel numb like the open ocean
Vast and deep
Far and wide
Yet nothing quite touches it.

It is like being sucked into a whirlpool
Unable to get out
Unable to stop
The feeling of nothing as deep as despair

I want to feel something
But the ocean within is as deep as can be
The vast hole in my heart keeps growing
As fast as the raging sea

If I could just place my thumb
On this feeling of numb
So that I can breathe again
Like the trees in the sun

@Bal.kaurc

UNSPOKEN

UNSPOKEN THOUGHTS
UNSPOKEN WORDS
UNSPOKEN FEELINGS
UNSPOKEN MEMORIES
UNSPOKEN ENDINGS

Amrit

Finding yourself again

She rose up

Like a phoenix

Not because she wanted to

But because she had no choice….

She must think about herself

Once more

She had to reclaim her power

Once more

She needed to know

Once more

What it was like to be

Her… once more

Not for anyone else

But for herself

@Bal.kaurc

Do not cry

Do not cry mummy

I am watching you, I will not know what to do

Do not cry daughter

I am watching you, all I want is for you to be happy

Do not cry wife

I would not know how to help you, I do not have the answers

Do not cry human

You are wearing all the hats, that need you to stay afloat

Do not drown in your tears, leave them for another day

The downpour of her tears drenched the pillow!

@Bal.kaurc

BE BRAVE

Believe

What is right?
What is wrong?

Am I right or am I wrong?
Is she right or is she wrong?

We are all one.
We are all mums.

No one is right.
No one is wrong.

Believe in yourself.
Believe in your baby.
Believe in your motherhood journey.

No mum is perfect.
No baby is perfect, but

Your baby is perfect for you.
You are the perfect mum for your baby.

Kim Saini

<u>Finding peace in motherhood</u>

I find the peace within me
And then it is gone
I am left searching again!

I feel like crying
But then I just hold it in
Left heavy once more

I find peace within
And then it is gone once more
Left searching again

@Bal.kaurc

I know its hard Mama

I know its hard Mama..

You feel so overwhelmed by all these new responsibilities...You feel so alone and unsupported. Remember, just because you are struggling, you are never failing.

You feel completely exhausted and you are tired of being tired. The lack of sleep is pressing on your emotions. Remember, just because you are struggling, you are never failing.

You feel you have begun to lower your expectations about what you can accomplish in a day. Some days consist of sitting in Pyjamas and constantly feeding. Remember, just because you are struggling, you are never failing.

You feel you are doubting yourself, you doubt your ability to be a good mother and you allow the tears roll down your cheeks. Remember, just because you are struggling, you are never failing.

You feel like your days are long. Your days are testing and your days are also so rewarding. Yet you know you need a break. Remember, just because you are struggling, you are never failing.

Jamie F.

A JOURNEY

You and Me

We've had quite a journey, so far, you and me
Since our little family became a three.

Eagerly anticipating, I watched you grow,
The feeling and connection, only we will know.

I held you close, until you were ready to be free,
And then the next chapter started, for you and me.

It was hard at first. Vulnerable, lost and a little confused,
My body and mind, battered and bruised.

But you were with me, and my heart was bursting,
Holding you close, mellowed the aches and the hurting.

And then it got easier, we worked out how to be,
We had found our groove, you and me.

Now here I am again, eagerly watching as you grow,
Thinking of all there is for you to experience, to learn, to know.

Bittersweet moments, you're growing up fast,
Swelling with pride, but wanting each moment to last.

So I'll make sure to pause, to stop and just be,
As we build our memories together, you and me.

TK

Protector

They say when a baby is born,
A mother is also.
I agree this is definitely the case
When I held you in my arms for the first time
And saw your delicate face.

As I absorbed your little features
This new mummy made a promise to herself
I would protect you with my life
And create our own little bubble
To keep you safe from any trouble or strife.

From the dark and lonely nights
Of rocking you to sleep.
To wiping away those tears
When you tumble and get a graze.
I will always be here to comfort you
And chase away those fears.

I love the way your little hand
Always reaches out for mine.
We will always be entwined together.
I know you look up to me to protect you
And this I promise to do forever.

As the years move on
And I watch you change
I see that you have grown
You are such a kind and loving soul.
With whatever life has thrown.

I feel my heart is walking out of my body
As you walk, skip and jump along.
You are following your own path
With me behind you all the way
I'm finding it hard to let you go
Its leaving me feeling in such disarray.
I look down to reach out to hold your little hand,
I search and it can't be true.
Your hand no longer searches for mine
And this breaks my heart in two.
Our fingers may not be interlocked
But our hearts will be connected for ever.

So as I walk with you side by side
I look down upon your face.
I see you moving forward
At a slightly quicker pace

I know I must you let spread your wings

And let you search the world.
But I keep my promises, my darling
Which I will never let slip.
The promise to be your protector
From things that may cause you to trip.

So as you go on your journey
Please don't forget to look back.
Your mummy will always be with you
Always ready to help you on your track.

You are my whole world
My life line and savior.
And I your mummy, with my arms open ready.
For I am your protector and ally.
But I promise you this my darling
And that is to let you fly.

Sareena Sinda
Mummy to Ishika Sinda

Never Give Up

Finally, I have that feeling, one I thought I would never feel,

The feeling that we are now complete, after the struggle to get here was real.

All I ever wanted in my life, was to become a Mum,

We tried and tried so hard, but it's really not that easy for some.

9 years ago it began for us, but it wasn't meant to be,

Everything was about to change, as our niece joined our family.

We fought long and hard through assessments, to persuade them she should stay,

Then in court the best thing happened, we became her legal guardians that day.

She made me a Mum and taught me so much, I was devoted to someone so small,

She changed my life forever for the best, I felt like I had it all.

But deep down I knew I still longed, for a bigger family,

Someone else to play with and a little friend, so she had some company.

IVF we were told, would likely be the only way,

This made me so sad but I just hoped, it would get us there someday.

And IVF isn't easy, in fact it can be very tough,

Another day and another injection, made me feel like I'd had enough.

Then after that I didn't expect, that I would then miscarry,

That hit me hard, I was so excited, how could this happen to me?

Then not long after, it happened again, was this even for real?

Brought me so much heartache and pain, that I thought I would never feel.

But after the storm they say, will come a big rainbow,

We gave birth to our first son, such an amazing feeling as you know.

With 3 frozen embryos left, we knew we wanted to have one more,

But all we had was a further miscarriage, and 2 embryos that failed to thaw.

What would we do now? Was it over? Was this really how it was meant to end?

Do we just give up or try again, even though it would be a lot to spend?

I knew if we didn't try just once more, I would always wonder what if we had?

I just had to go through it again, everything crossed the outcome not sad.

Then finally we welcomed into the world, another baby boy,

That feeling that we had finally made it, brought me so much joy.

I feel so blessed to be able say, we now have a lovely family of 5,

They mean the absolute world to me, as I watch them grow and thrive.

I don't think I will ever be able to shut out, the pain that we all went through,

But what I feel now is perfect, and where determination got us to.

I will never forget our little ones, that just weren't meant to be,

But look at what we have now, I really couldn't be more happy.

Bev

A FATHER'S LOVE

Being a Papa

Being a Papa is mad,

The news of pregnancy with my love made me glad.

10 weeks too early, changed thoughts from good to bad

Through the storm, more ups than downs with my lad.

I'm approaching my second father's day

It's been a crazy journey with more on the way

Got my wife by my side, my soul mate, the old cliché.

G's got us both feeling like were flying today.

Times changed so we're sitting sipping cabernet,

We come from our fathers, fathers that's what I say,

Sit & think about my Nonno & reminisce before the memories fade away.

His words would always be serious but with a smirk to let me know he just play,

Saying something like *EH, 'not scratch the blue chevrolet'*

Enjoy being a parent it's by far the sweetest of all trade

In a world where we need to understand to grow and teach them by what we display.

Simon Bonadies-Stefanoudaki

Only we can relate

The Love shows when I walk through the door.
You hug me around my legs until we fall to the floor.
Being greeted like this every day, is never a chore.
I get lost in these moments as if time is no more.

The time I invest into your interests are clear.
From painting my toes to Pokemon Go.
Fixing your wifi and giving you my ear.
You put stones in my pocket on our walk
or calling me Arthur when we talk.
Having eyes of a hawk when we play.
The special time we have on your Birthday.

Now when I walk through the door, I just get a hi.
You've grown in a blink of an eye.
You show your Love in an older way but I still wish you hugged me like you did back in the day.
I am the best father I can be.
Although there are days my children will not agree.
When they grow and reflect, they will see.
They truly get the best of me.

Stuart Mardell

Strength

The strength to power on
The strength to stay strong
The strength when times get tough
The strength to be the rock

The strength for all the bedtimes
The strength to clear up all the toys
The strength to keep us entertained
The strength to get through the tears

The strength when you feel alone
The strength when you can't escape
The strength for keeping calm
The strength for being there

The strength for continually being amazing

Strength, otherwise known as being Mum

Hitesh Patel

A CHILD'S VOICE

My childhood

My childhood is great, you'll see just wait.
It was just me, then found out a baby await.
Just before my birthday he came,
Fun times and memories together
And things were never the same.
Doing well at school
And making parents proud
Dancing in Disneyland
And singing at the O2 loud.
Being a famous singer is my dream,
For now, helping around the house is what mummy needs.
Being a big sister is significant and fun,
Sometimes I feel like a mini mum.
Having fun in the park is the best,
Two brothers is crazy,
No time to rest.
My childhood is great
With more to come, I'll wait.

Layla Neilson

I Love You

Dear Mummy

You are the best.
Better than the rest.

Even though I've tried and tried
You'll pick me up because you're by my side.

I love you with all my heart.
I know that nothing will keep us apart.

I know that I am getting older
Every time the wind gets colder.

I might not always hold your hand.
But I will when I am really sad.

You give me cuddles when I am in bed.
I read a book to myself at night, but sometimes you'll read to me instead.

Love From
Ishika Sinda
Age 9

Thank you

I would like to thank all the parents and children who contributed such emotive poems and bought my vision to life with this beautiful book.

I definitely feel that putting pen to paper and writing down our thoughts and feelings can be a release from our hearts from any pain and suffering, this takes such courage and bravery to share with everyone.

I also hope these inspiring poems can fill your heart with joy when reading the wonderful words from each mother and fathers parenthood journey.

"And then there are stories that reveal the transformation of an ordinary person into an extraordinary one, because he or she had the courage to hope, the determination to think positivity, the ability to see the beauty in life, the strength to pick up the pieces and move on and the faith that life is nurturing, if one allows it to be so. – Jack Canfield

The profits of this book will be donated to the charity Bedfordshire Sands

Bedfordshire Sands is part of Sands, the stillbirth and neonatal death charity. Sands operates throughout the UK, supporting anyone affected by the death of a baby, working to improve the care bereaved parents receive, and promoting research and working closely with many different organizations to reduce the loss of babies' lives.

Charity registration number 299679

Printed in Great Britain
by Amazon